MW00875439

a child evacuee's story

Memories of World War II

Story and Illustrations by

John Conder

with a little help from his big brother, Stanley

For my family:

Marcus, Rachel and Ruth

Foreword

Dad has always been a story teller. I don't remember him using books to read us to sleep — only his imagination.

As all of his grandchildren have grown older, they understand that you 'lean in' when Granddad starts a story. Then as you 'lean out' you are left to wonder what percentage of it is true and what percent is 'embellished'.

We will never know about 'Panino the blind sheep'.

Dad wrote this book for me and my siblings, for us to understand his childhood — and also his unease with me and my family living so far away. (We moved to the USA in 1994 and took his first grandchild with us, then had three more!)

The note that follows is what he enclosed when he mailed me the pages for this book.

To my dear daughter
Ruth — to explain
my separation anxiety

Lots of love —

Dad xxx

During World War II in England, the evacuation of children — called 'Operation Pied Piper' — took place three distinct times to relocate children to places that were considered safer than those near big cities.

The first of these evacuations began on 1 September 1939. By January 1940, almost 60 percent had returned to their homes.

The second occurred in June 1940, after the Germans had taken over most of France. By the end of 1941, cities — especially London — became safer and children once again returned home.

But in June 1944, Germans attacked again, and over one million women, children, elderly and disabled were evacuated from London, and most were unable to return until the war ended in May 1945.

This is one child's story.

Becontree

Mum and Dad were sitting round the family radio with my Uncle Percy and Aunt Doll, looking at the wireless very seriously.

"Be quiet!" my big brother Stanley told me.

Soon after, Father stood up and said, "War is declared."

"We shall all have to fight them", Uncle Percy announced.

I asked if I would have to fight them.

Once again, Stanley said, "Be quiet!" Then he added, "Of course you won't fight them. You're only four."

I crossed my arms over my chest and furrowed my brow at him. Didn't he realise I was four and a quarter?

Shortly after we moved into 19 Woodward Road, Becontree, Essex, Mum had a dream of having our plain backyard made into a lawn with flowerbeds. Because she had come from Poplar, a bit of a slum in London's East End, this was something she never had as a child.

But because there was a war on, the garden would have to wait. Poor Mum! Instead, my dad built a rabbit hutch in which he housed four rabbits. Then he bought some wire and made a chicken run. Eight chickens went into that.

The next thing I remember is some men delivering a pile of corrugated iron sheets, and then Dad and Uncle Percy digging a big hole at the end of the garden. I thought we were going to have a fish pond, but the hole kept getting deeper and deeper. As he dug, Uncle Percy called from the bottom of the hole:

"Going down . . .
kitchen ware . . .
ladies
underwear . . .
going down . . .
Australia . . .
New Zealand!"

Uncle Percy sure could make us laugh!

Dad had to work hard to fit the corrugated sheets together because some of them were bent, but when it was all fitted together in the hole, we shovelled earth onto the top and planted cabbages all over it.

It wasn't the lawn and flowerbed Mum dreamed of, but as I soon found out . . .

We weren't the only ones with this kind of garden.

Because people worried about food shortages during the war, everybody dug up their lawns and planted vegetables.

Even the park in our neighbourhood had potatoes and carrots planted everywhere. But that wasn't all . . .

There were also places for rocket guns.

Also, at the crossroads, men put up a tall post with a siren on top. They kept trying it out so that we would know when an air raid was on its way. It made a terrible wailing sound that was very scary.

Dawson Infants was the name of the school I went to. One day some men arrived with a load of bricks and built a shelter in the sports field. Then they brought a barrage balloon on a lorry.

When they blew it up, it was bigger than a house and coloured silver. It went up into the sky on a metal rope.

Lots of these balloons were sent up to stop enemy aircraft from flying over. If a plane did fly over, it would be sliced up by the wires.

One day our barrage balloon broke loose from the school and bounced across our back gardens, with its wires trailing behind it. The wires got tangled round the garden fences and picked up all kinds of things from our back garden.

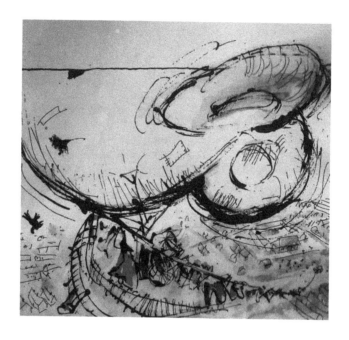

It was quite a sight to see the balloon dragging so many of our belongings towards the local pub, The Fanshawe. Once it reached the pub, it caught the wind somehow and blew up into the sky and away.

Stanley was the first to know that "evacuation" meant he was going to be sent away soon. His teacher at Bifrons School had given all the students a list of essential clothing to request from our parents.

"But we don't have most of these things," Mum complained. "Three shirts, three vests, three pairs of underpants, a warm topcoat." She shook her head as she read the list.

Stanley, on the other hand, had bigger things on his mind. He was building a huge model aeroplane using thousands of pieces of thin balsa wood and some thin sheets of balsa that he cut into shape.

When he stuck it all together, it really looked like a four-engine Wellington bomber.

THE BOMBERS FIRST & LAST FLIGHT

Stanley was told that he was going to be sent off the next day, so he rushed to finish making the plane. He had to stick on its paper skin, and while it was still wet with dope, we took it over the park to have its first flight.

"I'm being evacuated", he told me angrily.

I didn't know what 'evacuated' meant. Nor did I know that he had filled the aeroplane with cotton wool soaked with paraffin!

When he put a match to the cockpit and launched it high into the sky, the flames streamed out from the crippled plane, its wings folded, and then it hit the grass. Even the wreckage looked very realistic. There was hardly anything left except for a black patch in the grass.

It truly felt like an end.

Bradford
on Avon

Soon after that Mum, Stanley and I went with Stanley's school on a long train journey. There were lots of children on the stream train and it took ages to get to a place called Bradford on Avon.

When we arrived, we were sent to a large house at the bottom of High Street, where we were supposed to stay to be safe from the air raids and possible bombings at home. The house belonged to a doctor, but I never saw him, as we were told he was busy and should not be disturbed.

At the top of the street was a rubber factory. I always looked out to see if there were any rubber balls bouncing down the street, but never found any.

There was also a big bridge. Stanley fell off of it into the water and nearly drowned.

The house also had a cook and a maid. I remember the cook shouting at me because I was playing with some little insects that were swimming in the water. I had never been told off like that before.

My mother was unhappy in the doctor's house too.

One day, the cook told my mother to pick the ripe apples off the trees in the orchard. "You should hold them gently and give them half a turn," she said. "If they drop off into your hand, you should wrap each apple carefully and place it gently onto the floor of the attic, making sure they do not touch one another."

But Mum was tired of the cook telling us all what to do. So, after the cook went back into the house, Mum shook all the loose apples off the trees, then knocked down the remaining ones with her broom before dumping them into the attic.

Soon after that, Dad wrote to say there had been no air raids. What a relief! We were so happy to get on the train and leave the smelly apples.

Becontree

It was not long after we returned home that we had our first air raid and saw our first enemy aircraft. It was black and flew very low over our garden, so low that it seemed to block out the sky. I could see the crosses on its wings, as well as the pilot.

Stanley was eleven, and at his school the boys were taught how to recognise the different types of aircraft. Stanley said the man whose head we could see was the 'navigator', and that he and his crew were checking where we lived so they could come back and bomb us later.

I felt fear rise up in me as he pulled out his aircraft identity sheets.

"That one's called a 'flying pencil', he said. "They call it that because it's long and thin."

But that flying pencil wasn't the last plane I would see.

Soon after, a whole column of bombers, four abreast, came flying over the Thames towards the London Docks, with little fighter planes weaving from side to side over the long column.

Stanley said the fighters were protecting the bombers. Everyone complained that the Germans had the sky to themselves.

"Where is the Royal Air Force?" they complained. "Not a Spitfire or Hurricane in sight."

I was worried because my dad was an engine driver in the very place the bombers were heading.

You could hear the bombs exploding . . . crump . . . crump. The sky became as dark as night, so dark that the searchlights came on and swept the sky searching for aircraft.

If one was lit up, other searchlights would converge on it and the illuminated plane would be picked up by the next battery of lights as it moved across the sky. It sounded like all the guns in the world were shooting at it, but the anti-aircraft guns seldom seemed to hit them.

When Dad came home from work, he would tell us what had happened to him. One night, the raid was so heavy that he had to stop the ammunition train he was driving to take cover in a deep shelter. As he ran away from his bomb-laden train, he overheard some men sitting in a little trackside shed saying that they would be quite safe if they waited there.

When the siren sounded, usually at night, we would pull the bedding off the bed and run with it in our arms down the garden to the shelter. Inside, there was a night-light in a saucer of water. Stan said that it was in water so it didn't start a fire if it got knocked over. Dad said it was to reflect more light.

Devil's Coachmen were a sort of beetle that lived in the shelter. I would watch them climb slowly up the wall until it was almost climbing upside down. Once it got that far, it would fall onto our beds.

Sometimes we went to the public shelter to steer clear of the beetles, but Mum didn't like the community singing.

We were actually lucky. My friend who lived over the shops didn't have a garden. Instead of an Anderson shelter, his family had a Morrison. It was like a big metal table with wire mesh sides that they all had to squeeze into. Mum said she wouldn't be seen dead in a Morrison.

Once, we watched a 'dogfight'. The sky was very clear and blue, and there were lots and lots of fighter planes all circling around and chasing each other. It was like watching tiny toy planes. They whined and their guns made rat-tat-tat noises. And when the aircraft had soared way up high, they left vapour trails curling all round the sky. It was a stunning show.

One plane was hit, and the pilot's parachute opened and it started to float down. It began to swing from side to side like a sycamore seed. The plane trailed smoke, and I pointed it out to mum who immediately knocked me over and flattened herself on me. She only got off after we heard the crash.

One day, a spitfire got shot down and crashed into Spicers the greengrocers, leaving its tail sticking out of the roof.

Mr Willis, our neighbour who was a policeman, ran along the road towards the burning shop. Tracer shells sped out from the fire and bounced along the road.

I watched Mr Willis jumping up to avoid the shells. He was trying to blow his whistle and put on his jacket as he ran.

I could not believe that it was one of our planes. I thought only German planes got shot down.

Mr Comber was our headmaster. Every day he wore a black overcoat,
black tie, a bowler hat and pinstripe trousers, and he always carried a
wooden walking stick.

One day he showed us some pictures of a butterfly bomb, which he said was painted in bright colours to entice children to pick them up. He said that if we touched their wings they would blow us 'to kingdom come'.

After school, we went looking for butterfly bombs, but we couldn't find any.

Soon after we were told about the butterfly bombs, a pilot parachuted down into the Barking marshes. Some local men found him and, thinking he was the enemy, threatened to stick their pitchforks into him.

We heard that he quickly saved himself by telling them he was English. He probably said something like, "Bit of a prang, eh . . . Whiz-bang got me . . . Jolly bad show . . . Get the rotter next time."

Airmen, with their big moustaches, were all supposed to talk in funny-sounding little sentences like that.

Something called "The Blackout" was one of the oddest things we had to do. Everyone had to cover the insides of their windows with boards so as to stop any light being visible from the street. Neighbours would get very angry if someone showed even a chink of light. They said the Germans could see the flicker of a candle from eight miles away!

Even cyclists had to cover their lights so that they couldn't be seen. Unfortunately they couldn't see where they were going either!

The only way to spot a bicycle at night was by the white patches painted on their rear mudguards. Otherwise, they faded right into the blackness.

The A.R.P. men, a group dedicated to the protection of civilians from the danger of air raids, used to ride bicycles around the streets, blowing their whistles furiously if they saw a glimmer of light. Then they would shout, "Put out that light." It must have really been quite dangerous, as cars also had their headlamps shielded so that they couldn't see or be seen.

PLACE NAMES WERE PAINTED OVER

Another frustration was that all the place names had been blotted out or erased so that nobody knew where they were. On long train journeys, there was just one station after another, with all the nameboards removed. They even carved the place names off war memorials and other landmarks.

I think they did all this erasing of names so that spies would get lost and have to ask the way. Then they would get caught because of their German accents. It must have been very difficult for the Americans and all the other foreign soldiers who were camped in Britain trying to help win the war.

As you might imagine, England was full of people moving around, and nobody could tell where they were!

Dad came home one morning and said that something was wrong. He had heard about fighter aircraft that seemed to be damaged and then crash, causing a terrific explosion.

The rumour was that they may be a new German secret weapon — a flying bomb. Later we heard that they were named 'V1', but people preferred to call them 'doodlebugs'.

One day we were in the garden when we heard what sounded like a sick aeroplane. We saw it flying quite low, with flames pulsing out the back.

Mum looked up and put her hands to her face.

"The poor pilot . . . the poor pilot . . . the poor pilot", she cried out.

Dad shouted, "Run, you silly moo . . . it's a flying bomb."

It flew on to explode with a huge bang. That was the first
doodlebug we saw, but there were going to be many more.

Aunt Doll lived at number 33 Lochnagar Street, Poplar. Mum took me once to visit her after a raid there.

As the train got near to Bromley-by-Bow station, it went past some gasworks. It was still smoking and all the gas holders were bent or blown away.

Walking down from the station, we saw that everything was bombed. Lots of wrecked buildings and mountains of rubble were piled in the street. It was so dusty that I couldn't open my eyes.

Mum held my hand. When we got to Lochnagar Street, she said I could open my eyes. We saw that number 33 was okay, but that something had gone right through the house next door. The house opposite had vanished.

Its roof was blown away and there was a big hole through the ceilings and the floors, and there were no doors or windows. The people were inside looking for their things.

Inside Aunt Doll's house there was a hole in the wall behind granddad's chair. I knelt down and called through the hole to the boy next door, and we talked to each other. I was happy to hear that he was alive.

some of the hospital beds were hanging out over the street, with their sheets blowing in the wind.

Later, we went for a walk to find Aunt Doll's friends. In Brunswick Road, opposite the dock gates and Blackwall Tunnel, was Poplar hospital. The front wall was blown away and you could see inside it just like a doll's house.

Several of the floors were simply hanging there as though they were waiting to fall into the street.

The hospital beds, especially the ones on top whose sheets were blowing in the breeze, appeared ready to slide away.

I remember wondering what happened to the patients who had been lying in these beds.

It seemed impossible that they would have survived.

Silverton, Devon

Some weeks later, Stan's school got evacuated again, and I was sent away with him to a village in Devon called Silverton.

After we arrived, we were given a label to tie onto our coats in case we got lost, along with a paper bag that held a sandwich and an apple. We could sense that it was going to be another long journey . . . and it was.

We first went by train from London to Exeter, and then by bus to Silverton. When we got off the bus, we were lined up against the wall of a school where we waited for someone to choose us.

Girls were always picked first, so we were the last to be chosen because we were two boys. That's what Stanley said anyway. He insisted that someone would have picked him by now if it was not for me holding things up.

I'LL TAKE THIS ONE. HE LOOKS SWEET

When almost all the children had been chosen, a very old lady with a stick came along. She looked like a witch and poked at us. "I'll have these", she said. The lady in charge — called the billeting lady— asked where she lived so she could write it down.

"Number one, Condemned Cottages", The old woman said. It didn't sound very hopeful.

Darkness was falling when the old woman led us down a lane to her little cottage. It was made of mud and thatch, and it was very dark inside, with only an oil lamp or a candle to light a room. Lucky for us, the billeting lady came to check on us and soon moved us away to one of the council houses.

Our new home was called Lily Lake. The lady who lived there had a husband who was away at the war. She must have been very lonely, because she went dancing with soldiers almost every night.

I used to watch her getting ready to go out. Her body was very white, but she spent a lot of time putting powder on her face and shoulders. She reminded me of one of those dolls with a pink china head and white body.

I was fascinated by all the straps it took to tie up her underclothes and stockings. I guess she didn't mind them because smiled at herself in the mirror the whole time.

I once heard her talking with some other women who said that evacuees poo in the wardrobe. I was appalled! I was an evacuee and I didn't do that . . . but hearing that made me wonder if I should have.

We evacuees and some of the village boys used to run wild.

One very old man wore a sack over his head as he cut the field hedges. We weren't sure if he was trying to frighten us, or if he was just protecting his head. Nonetheless, we nicknamed him "Old frosty face" because he looked scary.

While he worked, we would creep along the other side of the hedge and suddenly all jump up.

"Old frosty face . . . old frosty face", we would jeer.

He would stand and raise his sickle and send us all off running.

He probably thought he startled us, but we were laughing the whole time.

Ya Boo - Ya Boo to frosty face - Tee Hee

When my mother came to visit and saw our home situation, she decided that living with the China doll lady simply wasn't good enough.

She immediately took me by the hand. "There has to be a better place for you boys", she said. "Let's go."

With that, we embarked on a search all through the village for better digs.

When we came upon the butcher's shop, my mother had a thought: that there would probably be more food for us if we lived with the butcher's family. She asked the man up front if we could possibly stay there.

The man looked us up and down. "You'll have to go to the back so they can check you out", he said, directing us to a doorway behind him.

I followed Mum through the butcher's shop and into the back room, and who was sitting at the table but old frosty face!

We kids had never been close to the butcher shop to see that it had a sign that read:

G. FROST,
FAMILY BUTCHER

We couldn't believe it! His name really was Frost! And even more unbelievable is that Stan and I ended up living there for the next two years.

Soon after we moved in with the Frosts, the German bombers came and bombarded Exeter. Once again, we heard the crump, crump of heavy bombs exploding across town.

A little house in Silverton came down the same night. I think that it fell down in sympathy. The cottages were made of cob, a sort of trodden clay and straw.

Mum used to like going on long walks, and one day when she came to visit us, we walked all the way to Exeter. When we arrived, we were shocked to find that in one night, the Germans had smashed it to pieces.

I couldn't help but feel like the Nazis were following me personally. I had believed that if you did something wrong, you would get punished, but I couldn't think of anything I had done so wrong that someone would want to try to kill me.

Mum and I were in the Frosts' shop one day when some ladies said there had been an invasion on the coast. One of them said it was at Sidmouth. The other said she heard it was at Budleigh Salterden.

It turned out to be just another rumour, but when I turned to Mum and said, "Mum, we're losing this war, aren't we?" She put her hand over my mouth, so that nobody else would hear what I said.

I learned that you mustn't say that sort of thing, even if you thought it.

"I CHOSE THE SAD ONE, WITH THE BIG EYES"

Mr George Frost always wore wellies and had a cigarette dangling from his lips. He was not only a butcher but also a farmer, with ten cows, several pigs and chickens, two horses, a tractor, some cats, two dogs, and a goat.

Mr George drove the tractor and went to market, while Mrs Frost looked after the shop. Miss Daisy was Mr George's sister who drove the little delivery van, and Granddad Frost milked the cows, groomed the horses, and hedged. I loved Granddad.

One day, Mr George took me to Tiverton market and let me choose a calf to buy. I chose the sad little one with the big eyes. I wanted to call it 'Favourite', but Mr George thought I shouldn't give it a name.

The next day, I found out why when I saw Mrs Frost putting pieces of Favourite in the sausage-making machine!

Sometimes I helped in the yard by washing out the chitterlings. These were the things pigs had inside them that looked like hosepipes.

I would put one end over the spigot and turn the tap on full. As you might imagine, the muck would gush out of the other end and spray all over the yard.

Sometimes it would spray one of the dogs that was out in the yard with me. The dog would shake it off, sometimes spraying me back.

That was good fun!

And Mrs Frost appreciated the help. She used the clean pipes for sausage skins.

58

I used to like watching Mr Frost cleaning and oiling his guns. He explained to me that one of his guns was a special pistol he used to kill the farm animals.

That sounded brutal, but I guessed they had to die for our food somehow.

One day, Stanley went with Mr Frost to visit a man who kept a pig. It was a pig intended for food, and poor Stanley had to hold the pig while Mr Frost shot it in the head. Then Mr Frost cut the pig's throat and Stanley had to hold the bucket to catch the blood.

Stan liked Mr Frost, but he said he didn't feel the same about him after that.

Stanley would sometimes work in the fields and help making haystacks. At harvest time everybody helped — except for me. I wasn't strong enough to stack stooks, but I did know how to do it.

The combine harvester was pulled round the edge of the field first and gradually worked towards the middle where the rabbits were.

When it reached that point, the rabbits would all run for it, with a little help from the dogs and everybody chasing them away with sticks, trying to club them.

One evening, Stanley was harvesting late and we waited up for him until it was quite dark.

Eventually, he came stumbling home.

It had been very hot, he said, and he and the men had worked, then had a sip of cider, then worked some more, then took another sip.

After all that work with so much cider in between, Stanley had come home rolling drunk!

63

With all our moving around, I had missed a lot of schooling, so I was worried about starting in the village hall. While waiting in the queue outside, one boy asked me if I had learned my tables.

"A bit", I said.

He said that twelve times twelve was "one hundred and forty four". That scared me.

There were three classes in the wooden hall. We little ones had the middle part by the stove. The other classes were at either end of the hall.

The first lesson was writing. Teacher told us to fill our slates with the letter 'a'. I chalked a very big letter 'A' with its roof right at the top of the slate and its two legs going to the bottom corners. I finished first, while the others kept on chalking.

I felt relieved that all the other children were slow . . . until the teacher told us to hold up our slates. They had all filled them with rows of tiny neat letters. I felt so stupid I cried.

I was determined not to be the kid people made fun of. I couldn't read yet, but I used to feed the hens and collect their eggs while we lived at Silverton.

One day a bicycle arrived, painted shiny black with my name and the butcher's shop address tied to the handlebars. Dad had bought it and "did it up for me".

Stanley took me out into the middle of the road and stayed close to me until I learned to balance the two-wheeler.

Not only did I learn to ride a bicycle, but later at school, I learned to read.

Not long after that, looking over Mr George's shoulder, I realised that I could even read his newspaper!

Mum came to stay with us because of the bombing. She did not know what to do at first, so she kept giving me a bath.

I must have been the cleanest boy in England.

Mum soon got a job helping the vicar's wife. The vicar and his wife were starving because she did not know how to make delicious meals out of scraps like Mum did — she could even make an Irish stew out of stale bread!

Mum did not mind scrounging, and I learned to ask Mr George for bones or pigs' tails.

Daisy sometimes took me on delivery rounds in her little van to other farms and villages. In the back doors, where there should have been windows, there were oval holes. One of the dogs would come with us and poke his head out to look for rabbits. If he saw one, he would leap out onto the road and chase. Sometimes, if we were going too fast, he would roll over when he hit the road, get up, and then start chasing again.

One day Miss Daisy got a letter. It said that her boyfriend was dead. She started wailing. Lots of people came around to see her, but they couldn't stop her from crying.

Once, when my brother and I were on a walk, a very old couple invited us into their dark little cottage. They both seemed very hairy.

The man wanted to show us some huge, ancient books he had. He lit a candle and opened a page so we could see where it prophesied the end of the world.

"The world will soon be ended", he said. "And even if you are very good, we will all be dead in no time."

My eyes grew large. He said this would happen by weeds taking over the earth — they were going to grow so big that they would strangle us. He said that it had already started with weeds on their way up the rivers.

He took Stanley and me into his garden, which had a little stream at the bottom, and sure enough we could see the weeds.

Sometimes Stanley would go off and nobody knew where he was. Later, we found out that an American couple called the Robertsons had been missionaries in France, where they had an orphanage for French and Jewish children. When the Germans came, the Robertsons claimed that they were one big family.

There were about twenty children between ages eight and eighteen. They all moved into a big house called Livinghayes, which stood on a hill outside the village.

Stanley found it and claimed that he went there because they had swings and orange juice. The truth was that he sneaked over there because of the girls, even though he couldn't speak French.

When the Robertsons found out that an outsider was visiting their children, they were quite pleased and invited us all to come to their Sunday school. The following weekend, a group of us eagerly showed up.

"Look out the French windows at the big dark spreading trees at the bottom of the lawn", Mr Robertson said. "Those are cedars from Lebanon, where Jesus came from."

He showed us a picture from the Bible where a father was going to stab his son, who was lying naked on a butcher's block just like Mr Frost's. The father's name was Abraham and his son looked like a skinned rabbit.

That story bothered me, even though Abraham changed his mind. When I told Mum about it, she said that when I was born, the doctor held me up by my feet and I looked like a skinned rabbit too!

Each weekend, we went to Sunday school at Livinghayes and were given a text to take home and learn, then recite to the class the following Sunday. I was younger than the others and found it hard to learn my verses.

One psalm in particular gave me trouble. It started, "The Lord is my shepherd who I do not want. He makes us lie down in wet fields."

Well, it was something like that!

Stanley enjoyed going with the Robertsons round the village collecting food or money for the orphans. He even joined their choir, but since they sang in French, he could only mime.

Eventually, though the war was still on, things had calmed down a bit and London wasn't being bombed anymore. So Stanley and I said goodbye to Mr and Mrs Frost, and to Granddad and Daisy, and got on the train for London to return home.

But this was not the end of the story . . .

Becontree

It was good being home again.

The rabbits and chickens were still there, and Mum still boiled up buckets of potato peelings and cabbage stalks on the cooker (for the animals, not for us). It was great to see Dad, but he was on shift work, so he sometimes didn't come home until breakfast time, then went to bed.

The children who had been evacuated gradually arrived back at school, but they seemed different. We had all been in new places, learning to live with strangers, and we all had stories. We also had heaps of new games.

We played touch, hide and seek on the playground (though the only place to hide was behind the dustbin), gobs, marbles and conkers.

But our favourite was flicking cigarette cards. The one that landed closest to the wall was the winner, and the best part was that you could build up a collection.

The big boys had their own games. One of them didn't look like fun at all, but they seemed to like it.

One boy was chosen as the buffer and stood with his back against the wall. The first team all bent down with their heads between the legs of the boy in front of him, then the other team jumped on them one after the other until they all crashed.

We had also had something called Empire Day, when everyone went to school in their uniforms: Cubs with their scarves and toggles, Lifeboys with their blue jumpers and badges. The Woodcraft Folk had a uniform too, but I can't remember now what it looked like.

The upshot of it all was that we had fights between the groups when we got to school . . . which were carried on at break time . . . then lunchtime . . . then afternoon break . . . then ended with us chasing each other all the way home.

I guess you could say it was the younger kids' version of the big boys' crashing game.

All us kids seemed to find endless places to use our imaginations.

Our local clinic had been bombed and destroyed, but it was a good place to play. We found a small parachute and took turns holding on to it while we jumped off the roof. It was a great idea, except that it didn't seem to slow our fall much!

Mr Comber saw me jumping off the roof and told me to come to his room the next day. Uh oh. I didn't want to go but I knew I had to.

For 'being reckless' he gave me the cane. Well . . . he didn't really give it to me so much as give me a whack with it.

It didn't really stop me from getting into mischief, though.

Another game we played was called 'being buried alive'. It involved digging a hole big enough for about four of us to crouch down in. Then we put up posts at each corner.

The next bit was to find boards and stuff to make a roof with. When this was ready, we collected as much rubbish as we could pile on top.

The game was to sit inside and pretend that there was an air raid, and that bombs were falling. To make it realistic, we would shake the posts until dirt would start falling into our hair . . . then bits of wood and stones.

We would keep shaking the posts until the whole lot collapsed and fell down on us. Then we would have to scramble out. If you didn't make it out, you were 'buried alive' and lost the game.

What fun!

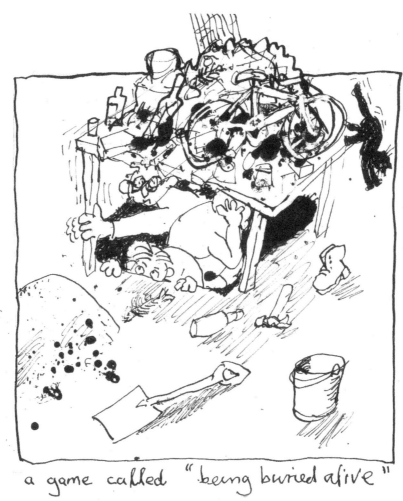

a game called "being buried alive"

We still had to take our gas masks with us wherever we went. Also, everybody had ration books, and when you bought something in a shop, the shopkeeper would cut out one of the little coupons to show that you had taken your weekly ration.

Food was in short supply and children ate everything that was on their plate, even if they didn't like it. Once, when Mum put the family's weekly ration on the table, she looked at the tiny amount and started to cry.

We began to get some really odd things to eat. Friday had always been the day when people ate fish for dinner. Now there was no fish, but we did get lumps of whale meat. Even Mum couldn't make that stuff taste of anything except oily cotton wool. Spam, though, was quite nice, along with powdered egg. Kids under five got special thick orange juice that came from the USA. Oh, how delicious that was!

Friday was also bath night. For me, this involved sitting in a tin tub on the living room floor, and having the water topped off with hot water from a kettle. Not fun!

Monday was wash day, which meant we only had clean clothes once a week. I bet we smelt! Sometimes we would help Mum at her scrubbing board, or with turning the mangle handle. That was definitely more fun than the baths!

Clothes were rationed, and mostly in short supply. But sometimes, there was a sudden glut of things — like the time there must have been an oversupply of long fishermen's socks. We had to help Mum take them apart, and then she would re-knit them into jumpers.

Perhaps the funniest thing was how Mum managed to get some parachute silk, which she used to make shirts on her sewing machine.

Although she made great effort, the buttonholes never worked, and the shirttails never stayed tucked in. When I went outside, the shirt would billow, like it wanted to be a parachute again.

Mum tried to improve the shirts by dying them different colours. When it rained, however, the colours ran and I would finish up a streaky red, blue, or green!

Dad had always mended my shoes, but now that the war was on, he couldn't get the leather. Instead, he cut strips from the treads of old tyres and nailed them onto the soles of my shoes. This made for an interesting bouncy walk!

It was also challenging during our very cold winter. Because food was scarce, we had to eat our pet rabbits. Afterward, my Dad stretched out the skins and sewed them together to make a piece of fur. Mum then sewed it into a pipe shape with the fur inside. The idea was for me to use it as a muff to keep my hands warm.

I didn't mind having Technicolor parachute shirts, or even bouncy shoes, but I wasn't going to school with my hand up an inside-out rabbit!

Even though the results weren't always the best, Mum and Dad were very good at 'make do and mend'.

At some point, Dad got the idea of turning empty bean tins into bunches of flowers. Mum cleaned the tins, while Dad cut and coiled the strips.

We cut petal shapes out of any decorated wrapping paper that could be found, and then fixed the flowers to the stems.

Mum took some to Barking market to sell for extra money.

ANGEL PLACE YOUNG MAN . THAT USED TO BE JUST THERE

Some wall posters told people to MAKE DO AND MEND, other posters warned us that WALLS HAVE EARS. This was to let us know that German spies might be listening to get our war secrets.

I didn't have any war secrets, but a man stopped me in the street and asked me the way to Ford Motor Works. That's where they made trucks for the army. The man spoke with a foreign accent so I knew that he must be a spy, and sent him in the opposite direction.

I then immediately ran off in case he came back to get me.

It was only afterwards that I realised he was probably an Irish man going to get a job.

I was seven by now and Stanley was fourteen. He had started work as a messenger boy in a place called Gracechurch Street in London.

Stanley had to find his way all round the city carrying bundles of paper called 'writs' tied up with red ribbon. He said that it was sometimes difficult to find the right office in the big buildings, especially with so many places in the city being bombed.

He told me that one day, travelling to work by train, the passengers were chatting or reading their newspapers.

"...its starting to dive"

Someone must have looked out the little bit of window that didn't have netting on it and saw a doodlebug flying alongside. The passenger looking through the spy hole gave a running commentary to the other passengers.

"Duck!" he shouted.

BBBBBBBB aaaaa nnnnnnggggggg

All the passengers crouched down on the floor until they heard the bomb explode. Then they all picked up their papers and continued reading, or carried on their conversations again, as though nothing had happened.

"Nice weather for this time of year"

Stanley was very surprised that everyone took it all so casually.

After the doodlebug incident, Dad wrote to the Frosts to ask if I could go back there, but another family had moved in and they were full up with evacuees.

So, we would lie in the Anderson shelter and listen to the doodles approaching. If they arrived overhead, you knew they would fly on to explode somewhere else, and we could begin to breathe again. If you could hear the engine stop before the doodle had arrived overhead, you would crouch in the silence and wait for it to explode nearby.

Once a doodle came and we could hear its engine going right overhead, so we started to breathe again. Something must have gone wrong with it because instead of flying right on in a straight line, it began to take a big circle and then come over us again!

The next night the siren went off again and as usual, we each collected our sheets and blankets from our beds and ran with the bedding to the Anderson shelter at the end of the garden.

Early in the morning, we were woken by an approaching doodle. When its engine cut out while it was still some distance away, we held our breath.

Seconds later there was a huge explosion that shook the ground so much that I banged my head on the wall. I scrambled out of the shelter in panic and saw a great smoke ring directly above my head in the dawn light. The perfect ring was still going up into the sky.

Mum followed me out, looked up and said it looked like a halo. I ran through the house and out toward the village, looking for the damage.

Behind our local shops was an allotment where people grew vegetables. In the middle of the allotment was a chapel that looked like a church, but it was made entirely from corrugated iron sheets.

The rag and bone man — who collected unwanted household items and sold them to merchants — had a horse-drawn cart, and he would tie the rein to a post near the chapel. After a day's work, the horse would rest and eat from its nosebag.

What I saw in the early light was that the chapel was no longer standing. Not one part of it was left except for the concrete pad where it had once been. Perhaps the eeriest part was that the horse was still there, eating from his nosebag, as if nothing had happened.

Another public shelter near our station was built around a huge old tree. One night, a flying bomb had crashed into the tree and then down into the shelter.

The big boys said there were still bodies down there and shut me in.

They let me out after I screamed a lot.

With all the bombings, Dad wrote to his sister to ask if she could take me in, as it was too dangerous in Becontree.

She agreed, and I had to put all my clothes and things on the double bed so that we could get away on the train early the next day.

Stanley couldn't come as he had to go to work.

We slept in the Anderson that night . . .

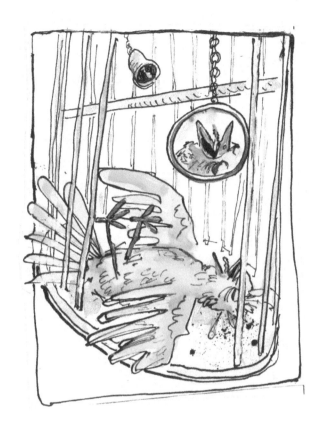

... and it was a good thing because we were all awakened by a big
BANG. When it was light, we went into the house and found a mess.
Glass and plaster were everywhere ... and the canary was dead in his
cage.

Upstairs it was even worse.

The windows had been blown in and the ceilings had been blown down — onto my carefully folded clothes.

It took awhile but we dug out the clothes and threw the rubble out the bedroom window . . . except that there wasn't actually a window there anymore, just a gaping hole.

I asked Dad why everything upstairs had been blown into the house, while downstairs, everything had been sucked out.

"A bomb blast does funny things" he said.

I didn't think killing my canary was very funny.

Lytham,
Lancashire

Dad took his dusty son on a long train journey to 49, St Andrews Road (North), Lytham St Annes Lancashire. The "North" made it seem even farther away.

The year was 1943 and I was eight when I moved in with Aunt Hilda and Uncle Fred near the seaside.

They had two girls: Eileen went to work and had a boyfriend, while Marion studied for her matriculation. She had long, curly hair and wore red flannel vests. I was put in Marion's room, and she doubled up with her sister.

I went to school, where I had no friends, and to church, where I was severely bored. Uncle Fred was a preacher at the Methodist Church. This meant I had to go to church on Sunday mornings, Sunday school in the afternoons, and to church again on Sunday evenings.

I remember light filtering through the tall coloured glass windows, and my uncle in the pulpit droning on to the silent congregation.

I would watch specks of dust floating down gently through the beam of light and changing colour as it drifted down.

Sometimes, if a person coughed, the speck would eddy upwards, settle . . . and begin its downward motion again.

Sunday was a non day and just had to be endured. It was also, by far, the longest day of the week.

When I moved to my aunt and uncle's house, I took my dolly with me.

He was made of blue velvet, and very soft, and he had big black buttons as eyes.

One night I had a nightmare and somehow managed to chew the ears off a rubber animal doll that Marion had left behind.

I said that I hadn't done it, as I couldn't remember doing it. So I got into trouble for lying, as well as chewing its ears off!

My uncle must have realised that I wanted friends, for he made me a fishing net so I could go fishing with the other boys. They all had bamboo sticks and neat nets bought from a shop. But mine was a big rough branch from a tree, and instead of having a net pocket at the end, it had a piece of shirt sewn to it. I was so embarrassed using that pole and net, even though my uncle said mine was far better than everyone else's.

MY NET WAS A LOT DIFFERENT

Our Sunday school room was used by Russian evacuees as their day school.

They put a big oilcloth map of the world on the wall. It had Russia, drawn as a huge red area, as the centre of the world.

Ha! We knew that Great Britain was the centre of the world! We had always been told it was a huge red empire upon which 'the sun never sets'.

And now the Russians had taken over our Sunday school and claimed to be superior. This led to big gang fights on the sand dunes. I joined in the fights until I was hit on the head by a piece of brick.

After that, my parents insisted I stay out of the rivalry.

Time passed slowly at Lytham-St-Annes.

Sometimes I went to the beach and would bring cockles back to the house to tend and feed before we had them for tea.

Other times I went out on Marion's bicycle, but it was too big for me, and I was scared of getting lost. One thing that bothered me was that I didn't know in which direction London was. It's not that I wanted to cycle home, but I did want to know the direction.

Food was still rationed, but Dad sent a parcel of six of our chickens' eggs each week. One day Aunt Hilda was cooking in the kitchen, and one of the eggs accidentally rolled off the table and smashed on the floor.

It was sad to see how she burst into tears.

On one occasion, Aunt Hilda took me to Blackpool. We had a great time at Pleasure Beach, and she let me go on rides. At the end of the day, we made our way back to the station, which was very crowded.

I had heard about a railway station where lots of people had been trampled to death in a stampede. It was mostly soldiers and men in uniform.

But we, too, got pushed and shoved and I couldn't hold on to Auntie. I could only see trouser legs and boots, and I thought sure I was going to be trampled. The crowd pushed me this way and that, and I couldn't even touch the ground with my feet. I kept screaming until an American soldier reached down and managed to get me onto his shoulders. I believe he saved my life.

Generally, though, we were a pest to G.I.s. (That's what we called American servicemen.)

When we saw them in the street, we would follow them.

"Got any gum, chum? Got any gum, chum?" we would repeat over and over, hoping they would give us a piece of chewing gum.

Sometimes they would give us a piece, then ruffle our hair like a friend might do.

Other times, they just shooed us away like bugs.

My only friend was a boy named David. He was a Jewish evacuee, and his dad had a pyjama factory in North London.

David lived next door, but we didn't go to the same school.

I would knock for David and ask if he could come out and play. We never did actually play very much. We would just walk alongside each other, and barely talk. I think he was homesick. Sometimes we just sat together in the park. There was a stone that was inscribed: "You are closer to God in a garden than anywhere else on Earth."

One day I knocked for David, and the woman simply said, "He's gone."

Uncle used to like reading the paper at breakfast time, and I would run off to the newsagents each morning to get it. I knew that if the war was over, it would be announced in the newspaper.

Sometimes if it was raining, I would be reluctant to go, and Uncle would say, "Don't you want to know if the war is over?" and I would run off.

The Daily Mirror had a cartoon each day of a woman called Jane. It almost always had Jane taking some of her clothes off.

Uncle Fred said it was for the troops, to 'boost their morale'.

All of us boys knew that if she had no clothes on at all, it would mean the war had ended.

But one night we saw something more disturbing than anything else we had seen. We went to the pictures, and in the newsreel, it had the British troops rescuing Jewish people from a concentration camp. They were all stick thin and moved slowly, and they all wore pyjamas. They showed piles of dead bodies like firewood. It was awful.

Becontree, Once Again

Soon after that, my dad came and told me that the bombing was over and took me home.

He told me about V2s, which were big rockets that travelled faster than the speed of sound, and how he had been at work in Stratford Junction when a V2 exploded directly in front of his steam engine. Dad thought he had been the nearest person to an exploding V2 and survived.

Stanley said that when he came home, he was white like a ghost, and had his eyebrows burnt off. The firebox of his steam engine had blown back, and he was caught in the flames. Even the metal footplate he was standing on had been torn up by the blast.

We heard that a lot of people had been killed who were much farther from the explosion.

Dad had been incredibly lucky.

But after that day, he never talked about it again.

The grown-ups always used to go on about what it had been like 'before the war' when you could buy oranges and bananas, eat sweets and go on holiday.

We had a map from The Daily Telegraph pinned to the wall, and each day we would read the war news and move some coloured pins to keep up with the armies advancing on Berlin. I hoped that the Russians would get there first, as I figured they would punish the Nazis more than the British or the Americans would.

I guess that I was an angry little boy.

I couldn't remember what oranges or bananas tasted like, or ever having the nice things my family said they had before the war.

Boys would bring interesting things to school that they had got from their older brothers who were soldiers or sailors. The school seemed full of German medals, helmets, flags and other things. I liked the guns best and managed to get a little black handgun, which had its spare bullets in the handle. My Dad asked Mr Willis what to do, and he took it from me. He later told me that he burned it at his work in a steam engine firebox.

Then I got hold of a silver six-shooter. I liked to take it all apart and then put it together again, and I liked the clicking sounds it made when the chamber was spun or the safety catch was set.

Somehow I let Dad see it, and off it went to Mr Willis once again.

Dad did let me keep a little red dingy sail that was about the size of six handkerchiefs. It had instructions printed on it to show how it should be used.

I wondered whether it would have been very useful in the North Atlantic.

Other boys took hand grenades to school, but they were all duds.

Soon, to everyone's relief and delight, the war was over and my mother took me to the Victory in Europe celebrations in London. There were crowds of us in the mall, and we climbed onto the Victoria Memorial outside Buckingham Palace.

Triumphant shouts filled the air. Eventually the King and Queen came out, and we cheered ever louder.

We saw the Queen disappear then bring out Princesses Elizabeth and Margaret to see the crowds. Then Mr Churchill joined them and they all waved.

When it got dark, we watched the men and women dancing in the streets.

We all went to a place called United Services Club where a lady came out onto their balcony and sang, "When the Lights Go On in London".

As she sang, the sky magically lit up as all the lights came on throughout the city.

It was a glorious sight to see, and a memorable night, indeed.

It also marked the end of a very tragic time in our world's history, one I hoped we would never revisit.

STREET PARTY - VICTORY IN EUROPE DAY - POPLAR

A Child Evacuee's Story

Text and illustrations copyright © John Conder

Published 2021

ISBN: 978-0-9982373-8-1

Printed in the UK and USA

chp
CONDER
HOUSE
PRESS

CPSIA information can be obtained
at www.ICGtesting.com
Printed in the USA
LVHW070403180621
690568LV00015B/1569

9 780998 237381